How the Small Business Administration (SBA) Evolved

(An example of how a government agency is created and evolves)

First Edition

Danny Wilson – Bachelor's degree for Sociology and Master's Degree for Public Administration Management

BookLocker
Trenton, Georgia

Print ISBN: 978-1-958892-60-2
Ebook ISBN: 979-8-88531-723-8

Published by BookLocker.com, Inc., Trenton, Georgia.

BookLocker.com, Inc.
2024

First Edition

Library of Congress Cataloging in Publication Data
Wilson, Danny
How the Small Business Administration (SBA) Evolved (An example of how a government agency is created and evolves) by Danny Wilson
Library of Congress Control Number: 2024908112

Dedication –

This Social Science book is dedicated to my family, friends, publisher and all of those individuals that believed in me writing and publishing this book for a Social Science, Sociology, Business, Political and Governmental example, and perspective of how an organization is derived, evolves, and succeeds going forward.

How the Small Business Administration (SBA) Evolved

Table of Contents

Preface —

This is a book that could provide academia and anyone in the areas of Sociology, Business, Political Science, Public Administration, Policy and Law an example of how a government agency is created, functions and evolves. I wanted to give a sociological, public administrative and business view into the details of how a government idea is born of necessity. I also wanted to give an example of how stresses and powers contribute to the character of an agency. In addition, I wanted to illustrate how an agency evolves, succeeds and sustains through changing times, to remain relevant.

This social science book is written from the perspective of an author that has a Bachelor's in Sociology and a Master's in Public Administration Management graduate. The author has also had experience working in both the private sector and government sector combined for over twenty-five years plus at the time of this publication. The author has completed research projects and admires the theory and related research of functionalism, in terms of how society has structure and order that can be researched using social science.

The sociological need aspect is at the heart of what a government agency or any agency/organization must be aware of on a daily basis. This will help them remain relevant. Thus, in this social science book, I wanted to depict that the need for an organization is the most importance factor for its existence and relevance, most of all. Thank you.

Danny Wilson

Social Science

From: The Academy of Social Sciences

Social Science is the study of people as entities, groups and societies. It is the study of their behaviors and interactions with each other and their created technologies, organization and environments.

Reference:

ACSS.org UK <u>What is Social Science</u> April 15, 2024
https://acss.org.uk/what-is-social-science/

Introduction

Danny Wilson holds three college degrees, including an Associate's degree in Liberal Arts, a Bachelor's degree in Sociology and a Masters's degree in Public Administration Management. He has worked for the private sector and for government. He has completed social science research experience using his degree training after gaining his Bachelor's degree in Sociology. This degree training was used to perform research for a government-mandated study of a community college. This was used to help secure funding for the college, while working at the college in 2001, receiving a thank you and recommendation letter from the Dean of Institutional Research/Academic Services dated 2003. He has had articles and small books published. He also has received several organization certificates for completed training for those organizations. These range from private to governmental organizations related to the Hospitality Business, Retail, Department of Labor assistance, State case working, and United States Navy military mechanical ship propulsion machinist service from his serving in the military. He has worked in the hospitality industry for over 9 years, occasionally assisting with business operations. He has done federal accounting assistance and has knowledge of public policy with a Master's degree in Public Administration Management. Some of his hobbies include creating art, cooking and of course writing for entertainment, government, social science and business.

In this social science book, the areas of interest will be as follows:

- How did the Small Business Administration first come into existence?

- Who were some parties or individuals that contributed to its existence?
- What value or need promoted the SBA as an element of social change, business assistance and governmental change?
- What were some of the realizations for its function to have relevance?
- What did it encounter as an example to the reader?
- Who did the organization first give services to, and did that evolve or change?

Most of all, I hope to introduce the reader to an example of how functionalism in social science, business and government maybe useful to know and maybe built upon, both today and in days to come if one wishes. I hope you find the book useful and enjoyable.

Afterword – In relation to functionalism, social science, business and public administration, I hope one has found this to be a great opportunity to see what institutions, organizations and social science can mean to the function of society. I also hope you see this as an example of how social science can be important to researching organizations as examples and more. Thank you.

Chapter 1:
Evolution of the Small Business Administration (SBA)

About SBA

The Small Business Administration (SBA) is an independent agency of the United States government tasked with serving, supporting, and protecting the interests of small companies. The SBA provides instructional resources to help entrepreneurs manage the complexities of business growth. It advises, counsels, assists, and protects small business interests. It ensures that small business concerns receive a fair share of government purchases, contracts, and subcontracts, as well as sales of government property. It makes loans to small businesses concerning, state and local development companies, and victims of floods or other natural disasters. It also may assist victims of certain types of economic injury. Along with this of course, it can help with licensing, regulating, and making loans.

What can the Small Business Administration do to help small businesses?

The SBA provides assistance and support through four key channels, many of which can assist small companies in their initial years of operation.

The four key kinds of services provided by the SBA are, one – Access to Capital, two – Entrepreneurial Development, three – Contracting and four – Advocacy.

Their functions include:

1. Access to Capital – The SBA provides a variety of financial types of resource to choose from.
2. Entrepreneurial Development – The SBA provides counseling and low-cost training for business owners.
3. Contracting - The SBA provides 23% in government contracts to small businesses, 5% to women Intrapreneurial business owners, 5% to small disadvantaged businesses, 3% to HUBZone small businesses and 3% to the disabled and veteran business owners.
4. Advocacy – The SBA advocates for businesses by reviewing legislation that pertains to all businesses, to protect them at all levels of the SBA's lawful ability.

If a company provides a service that the government requires, the Small Business Administration can assist it in *bidding for and receiving a contract to supply that service*. The government has a legislative goal of allocating 23 percent of prime contracting money to small business, which amounts to billions of dollars in small company contracts each year.

In 2023 the SBA delivered $50 billion dollars to different businesses.

The business applications illustration below is from a recent statistic of a Whitehouse webpage depiction and is provided by the United States Census Bureau.

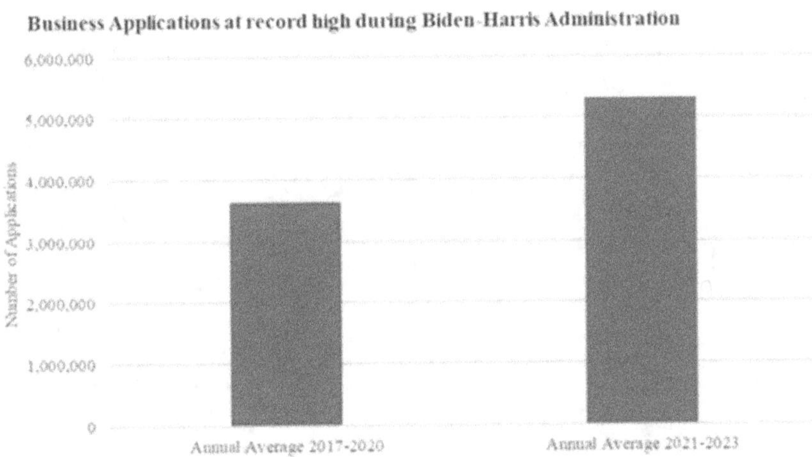

The business ownership illustration of Black and Hispanic households below is from a Whitehouse webpage as a depiction provided by the United State Federal Reserve.

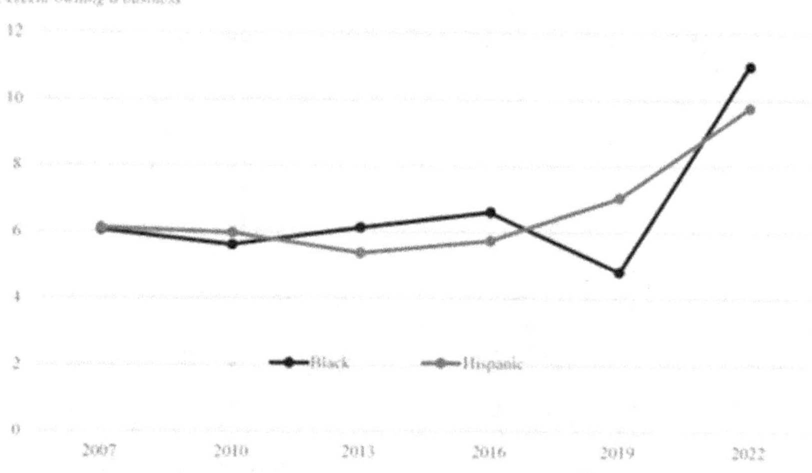

Even a small portion of that sum is sufficient to help many small companies survive, making this an invaluable opportunity for any company that applies. Small businesses frequently require capital, which is where the subject of access to capital comes in. This portion of the Small Business Administration services is dedicated to providing businesses with access to *various levels of funding*, ranging from one micro-transactions to two venture capital.

Given the simplicity of SBA service methods, many new companies prefer to handle their early needs through the SBA and only begin seeking money through other means once they've established themselves.

In addition to the two categories mentioned above, the Small Business Administration provides training for entrepreneurs, with a focus on education, counseling, and technical help for new businesses. Much of this development work is done for free, either online or in person, at one of the many SBA training centers. A few training sessions charge a small fee, but the cost is kept to a level that even small enterprises can afford. While large corporations have a lot of regulatory clout, small businesses are not left alone without clout. The SBA is frequently called before Congress to testify about how proposed legislation may affect small businesses. Because it is asked to testify, it conducts significant amounts of independent research that small businesses can use to get a better sense of their current environment. Through this effort it can help with efforts to overcome the challenges they face also.

The brief evolution of early change below states some of governmental efforts of the SBA during particular periods of need, as it evolved from its mission and creation.

Mission

The SBA's Economic Development Mission is to maintain a strong small business foundation for our nation's economy.

How The SBA Evolved: A Brief Background

The Small Business Administration (SBA) was founded in 1953. It was established to replace the position of the Reconstruction Finance Corporation (RFC), an independent US government organization whose principal mission had been to assist with the Great Depression.

Individuals in the banking industry were outraged by the RFC since it would use the banks' best lending assets as security. While the RFC helped supply liquidity, most bankers believed the price banks were forced to pay was far too high. Rather than just disbanding the RFC, then President Eisenhower established a smaller agency to assist small firms with their financial needs.

The SBA was established as an autonomous US government organization to assist small business owners and entrepreneurs. The government thought that by assisting entrepreneurs in establishing small firms, the SBA would help to sustain the US economy.

The United States economy and the Great Depression: The Reconstruction Finance Corporation was founded as a result of the economic impact of the Great Depression and the search for a remedy.

The RFC prior to the formation of the SBA had noted flaws. The RFC's continuous inadequacies led to it being disbanded. It was disbanded following claims of corruption and fraud also.

The SBA (Small Business Act): This is the current Small Business Activation, which was enacted in 1953.

In this informational history depicting the origins of the SBA, the SBA's origins, from the Hoover administration to the present act is presented as follows:

Predecessors:

1932

In 1932, in an effort to create better outcomes during the financial crisis that was brought on by the Great Depression, President Herbert Hoover established the Reconstruction Finance Corporation (RFC). The RFC was a federal financing program that was available to any company, no matter how large or small, that was in desperate need of financial assistance. Franklin Delano Roosevelt, who was then the President later, supported the RFC even more.

1942

In 1942, the United States Congress established the Smaller War Plants Corporation (SWPC) with the intention of assisting smaller companies in their ability to compete in the manufacture of war materials. Small companies were eligible for direct loans through the Smaller War Plants Corporation (SWPC), which also lobbied government procurement agencies on their behalf and urged other financial institutions to extend credit to small enterprises.

1945

Following the conclusion of World War II, the SWPC was dissolved, and the RFC took over its loan and contract functions. In addition, some of the tasks of the disbanded organization were taken on by the Office of Small Business (OSB) in the Department of Commerce. The OSB's primarily focuses was on providing education and counseling to business owners.

1951

During the time of the Korean War, Congress established the Small Defense Plants Administration (SDPA) in order to assist with issues pertaining to small businesses and to certify companies as being capable of fulfilling government contracts. By 1952, President Dwight Eisenhower had made a proposal to establish the SBA. This was done with the intention of continuing the functions of the RFC, which faced the possibility of being dissolved by Congress.

1953

The United States Congress established the Small Business Administration (SBA) in 1953.

1958

The Small Business Investment Company (SBIC) Program was designed to both regulate and assist in the provision of funding. This was for venture capital investment businesses that were privately owned and operated.

1964

The Equal Opportunity Loan (EOL) Program was established by the Small Business Administration (SBA) with the intention of easing the credit and collateral criteria for small firms whose owners lived below the federal poverty line, and are unable to attract sufficient financial backing.

The Small Business Administration (SBA) as of 2011, according to the Equal Employment Opportunity Commission (EEOC), had employed about 2,790 permanent employees and about 1,875 temporary employees. Considering remote working and other rules in 2024 this can change from day to day.

The SBA has at least approximately one Office located in every state, and a yearly budget of about 1 billion to operate. More than 52 billion in loans was delivered in fiscal year 2023 to business owners from its government institution also.

To highlight the SBA even more, in January of 2012, President Obama brought the Small Business Administration back into the Cabinet, a position it had not occupied since the days of the Clinton administration.

Milestones of the SBA

The Small Business Administration continues to assist small companies and entrepreneurs. It also reaches out to minority communities, women, and veterans of the United States Armed Forces. As a small business owner or aspiring entrepreneur, the SBA can provide you with specialist advice or support in expanding your trade beyond the limits of the United States. The SBA has been successful in assisting many small business owners in obtaining funds to expand their operations. While the SBA is not perfect, there is no doubt that many small businesses are still in operation because the SBA assisted their owners in obtaining the financial assistance they required, to bring the business into profitability.

The government's efforts to assist small enterprises through the SBA is indeed important to the country. Here one can see the numerous actions the US federal government has made. These guarantee that small company owners and entrepreneurs benefit from the SBA's assistance.   This includes the SBA's various programs, including loans, investments, surety bonds, federal procurement, foreign trade, and disaster recovery aid to name a few.

What to do to get SBA loan assistance:

Discover the steps to take while applying for an SBA loan. Find out what you need and what information your lender may require before offering you the loan.

The SBA can help you contact a lender, see what loan fits you and try to assist you in gaining your loan if you qualify.

An illustrated depiction below is from an SBA.gov webpage highlighting the loan process.

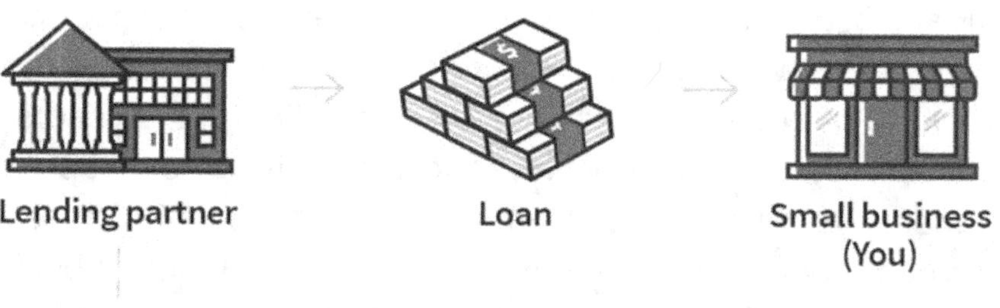

SBA reduces risk and enables easier access to capital.

The SBA Organizational Structure:

A description of the Small Business Administration and its organizational structure, including its various offices and locations can be found in many of its contact methods, such as its website at SBA.gov.

The SBA Website:

Contact the Small Business Administration on its website, its addresses and phone contact. Also, obtain tools and the most recent updates on loans and the agency's many programs.

Chapter 2:
Reasons for Creation

Why Was the SBA Established?

After the RFC was disbanded, President Eisenhower saw the need to assist small companies and enterprises in surviving the harsh economic climate generated by the Great Depression across the country. The SBA was established by an act of Congress. President Eisenhower signed the Small Business Act into law on July 30, 1953. The Small Business Administration was supposed to persuade banks and other private lenders to lend to small business owners and aspiring entrepreneurs. It would accomplish this by providing government loan guarantees. From its creation, the SBA was also mandated to provide direct loans to catastrophe victims, there by assisting them in their rehabilitation. Furthermore, the SBA was created to assist small firms in obtaining government contracts that had previously been largely reserved for bigger corporations.

In the economics of funding a small business the SBA provides a support to small businesses and can assist with funding. The SBA can help on gain a comprehensive understanding of how one can achieve a goal as a small business owner or entrepreneurs for SBA catastrophe assistance. One can discover how the SBA can assist disaster victims on their road to recovery. One way is through contracting.

Gaining federal SBA federal contracting:

According to the SBA they can assist you with 3 main areas for gaining a federal contract. They are:

1. The SBA can assist with contracting guidance.
2. The SBA can give contracting assistance through their business development programs.
3. The SBA can assist with counseling and help with understanding federal contracts.

The Basic Need for Creation:

Congress established the Small War Plants Corporation (SWPC), a predecessor institution of comparable historical significance, in 1942, during World War II. The SWPC was established in order to help small firms that were being shut out of receiving contracts for wartime defense, in contrast to the RFC, which was established to provide assistance financially. This program's supporting policy introduced new kinds of details that encouraged large financial institutions to offer loans only to small enterprises. The rules governing SWPC also permitted it to directly offer loans. Additionally, it encouraged big companies to hire small companies through contracts with federal agencies. The SWPC was abolished after World War II, and all of its authority was transferred to the RFC. The Small Defense Plant Administration (SDPA) was a new government agency founded during the Korean War. To ensure that small enterprises could manage contracts that will be awarded by the RFC, this administration qualified them for competency.

Chapter 3:
New Power of Protection

The then President of the United States, Dwight Eisenhower, made the suggestion to establish a small business agency in 1952, at the same time that the RFC was being disbanded. This concept served as the basis for the creation of the Small Business Act on July 30, 1953, which in turn led to the establishment of the Small Business Administration by Congress. The mission of this organization was made abundantly clearer than that of any other that had come before it. This new Small Business Administration was given a different type of protection power, in contrast to the other agencies that provided financial aid, certificates, and provision of contracts. The new Small Business Administration was given the authority to safeguard, aid, and assist businesses, to the greatest possible extent, to the best interests of the small business community. The policy of the Small Business Administration (SBA) is to ensure that small businesses receive a fair portion of government contracts, and will make it available for them to purchase surplus properties.

These objectives will be accomplished by the SBA as a result of the key programs and services it provides. The SBA will be better able to support small businesses in increasing their revenues and maintaining jobs as a result of opportunities to participate in government contracting and financial assistance programs. The Small Business Administration (SBA) will assist communities in the development of thriving entrepreneurial ecosystems by providing counseling and training services, as well as advocacy for small enterprises. Small companies and communities affected by declared disasters will get support from the Small Business

Administration (SBA) in the form of disaster assistance. The Small Business Administration will place emphasis on the ongoing development of processes and will base its decisions on outcomes and evidence. The strategic goals of the SBA include a number of objectives and initiatives that are directly related to the performance of the agency as a whole and of individual employees. The purpose of these goals, as well as the objectives and strategies contained within them, is to ensure that the millions of entrepreneurs and small business owners, who use SBA products and services each year, receive assistance in a manner that is both efficient and successful.

The SBA's purpose is to preserve and strengthen the nation's economy by facilitating the establishment and viability of small enterprises. This is also done by assisting in the economic rehabilitation of communities following disasters, with the power that have been assigned to the SBA.

The SBA Executes, Monitors, Evaluates, and Improves

Within the context of an extensive performance management system that the agency has in place, a Strategic Plan service is a primary guiding service. It is intended to permeate all levels of the organization and provide a synopsis of the methods that will propel movement toward the SBA's four strategic goals.

Each of the strategic goals has its own set of core strategic objectives, which are backed by a separate set of performance goals and a subset of agency priority goals. The strategic goals and objectives not only serve as an overarching guide for the allocation of resources, needed to accomplish the agency's desired long-term outcomes, but they also act as a guide for the achievement of the agency's strategic goals and objectives.

The staff of the SBA will use this Strategic Plan to translate strategies into actions and then translate those activities into results. The leadership of the agency will measure and review the progress made toward each aim on a regular basis. In addition, the responsibility of ensuring the achievement of each strategic goal falls on the shoulders of a senior accountable official who serves as the objective lead.

According to the webpage Guidant Financial, the SBA has 4 key steps in fulfilling their strategic goal to execute. They are:

1. The SBA helps you with Document collection and packaging them.
2. The SBA helps you with selecting a lender.
3. The SBA helps you with getting through the underwriting process and its completion.
4. The SBA helps you with closing your loan.

Key Protections are there to monitor Performance:

The administrator and the leadership team will use the framework provided by the Strategic Plan to establish the organization's priorities and strategies to monitor and evaluate events. Program offices participate in performance reviews on a quarterly basis in order to discuss their progress toward both the Performance Goals and the Agency's Priority Goals. The Small Business Administration (SBA) conducts an analysis of its strategic goals on an annual basis. By doing this along with conducting a review that provides a summary of the most important successes, opportunities, difficulties, and risks, using evidence and evaluations, it can make informed decisions.

The SBA's Office of Performance Management creates dashboards, which are then distributed to leadership in order to give support for the reviews and improvements. The Small Business Administration has a strong culture of performance management, which involves leadership at all levels of the business, and it adheres to the principles specified in the Government Performance and Results Act and Modernization Act of 2010. The Small Business Administration (SBA) keeps track of its performance accomplishments and difficulties through its annual performance plan and annual performance report.

To ensure that every worker is aware of the ways in which their contributions affect the agency, a performance plan is kept up to date for them. This is aligned with the strategic goals, and the objectives outlined in this Strategic Plan.

SBA Loan Industry

The market for SBA loans can be segmented into the following broad categories:

Large banking institutions such as Chase, Bank of America, and Wells Fargo generate the majority of their SBA loan volume. The banks do this by offering loans, particularly express loans and lines of credit, to customers who would not be approved for normal bank credit. This assistance is needed due to factors such as the amount of time the company has been in operation or slightly more stringent underwriting criteria. Banks, as opposed to other financial organizations, have highly developed computer systems that typically make this process simple. Because of this, banks have a competitive advantage over other financial companies that use SBA funding for unique and different aims.

Banks of every size make extensive use of Small Business Administration loans, in order to provide financing for the purchase or construction of business owner-occupied real estate. This is the sole reason that many banks provide Small Business Administration loans. In particular, they provide financing for properties that a conventional bank would view as being too risky to finance, due to the fact that they have a specific use (such as a bowling alley or an automobile repair shop). This could also be of an environmentally risky nature (such as storage for petroleum products or an electrical substation), both of which can limit the property's resale value at times. Motels, gas stations, and car wash companies are a few examples of types of properties that can be purchased.

Individuals are also encouraged to buy established businesses through the use of SBA loans. Because, in contrast to real estate transactions, commercial lenders are able to finance the referral fee. These are earned by business brokers who assist individuals in the buying and selling of businesses. This sector of the industry maybe supported by smaller banks and standalone finance companies that are familiar with the market.

Chapter 4:
Awareness and Bias

It's a common misconception that the Small Business Administration (SBA) initiates loans to businesses. In addition, the agency will guarantee a portion of the loans that are provided by partner financial institutions such as banks, credit unions, nonprofit organizations, and other types of financial institutions. In the event that the borrower does not pay back the loan, the SBA will reimburse the lender for any monies that were lost. As a result of the reduced risk associated with SBA-backed loans, financial institutions and other partners are able to provide more favorable interest rates, and fee structures. The terms and interest rates associated with SBA loans are typically the most favorable you'll find.

It is said that loans guaranteed by the government do not come without any drawbacks. SBA loans are notorious for having drawn-out application processes that need a significant amount of documentation. This is because they are the result of a collaborative effort between numerous institutions, one of which is the United States government. A lot of waiting is also required. It's also possible that not all small business owners are eligible for SBA loans, particularly those with less than stellar credit. You will still need to have a fairly strong borrower profile and be willing (and able) to wait a few weeks to get your funds. This is despite the fact that some SBA partners, such as Smart Biz, have found ways to speed up the process. This is the case even though some SBA partners have found ways to speed up the process.

The SBA provides its services in the following intricate ways:

Short-term Assistance

In 1954, the Small Business Administration began offering natural catastrophe loans in addition to its other lending options. These included direct loans and bank loan guarantees. It was running the following programs at that time:

Access to Capital Program

The United States Small Business Administration (SBA) receives a partial guarantee from the Federal Government for the loans that are provided through its partner banks, credit unions, and other lenders. They make it possible for small enterprises to obtain financing, even if traditional lending standards would make it impossible for them to do so. SBA loans and lines of credit can be used to assist businesses in starting up. This can help with expanding their operations, purchasing land or buildings, and/or purchasing already established companies.

The Disaster Relief Loan Program

This program offers low-interest loans to property owners, renters, businesses of all sizes, and the majority of private nonprofit organizations. This is so that they can replace or repair assets and property that have been harmed by a natural catastrophe.

Additional Services

In addition, the SBA collaborates with other organizations in order to acquire government contracts. This addition provides assistance with managements, offers technical assistance, and provides assistance with training in general.

Long-term Assistance

After four years, the Federal Reserve came to the conclusion that small business enterprises were unable to obtain the type of finance they required. This was to meet the challenges posed by the rapid growth of technology. They required support in the form of long-term loans, as well as equity for their venture capital investments. The Investment Company Act of 1958 was the solution to this problem. It provided the Small Business Administration the authority to monitor, license, and assist privately managed venture capital organizations. These are all put in place to help in the process of delivering financing.

The Investment Company Program

The Small Business Investment Company (SBIC) program was designed to stimulate and supplement the flow of private-equity capital and long-term loans to small businesses. This is generally those that are independently operated and do not have assets that exceed $9 million, for the purposes of growth, expansion, and modernization. To assist with this, the government provides the Small Business Investment Company (SBIC), which is regulated and licensed by the Small Business Administration (SBA). The SBIC can help with long-term loans at an interest rate that is approximately equivalent to the government's cost of borrowing, which is often between 7 and 8 percent. This was created in 1958 to assist with gaining venture capital and to create the growth of start-ups.

Services provided:

SBICs may make investments in small firms in the form of either debt or equity, or in certain cases, a combination of the two. This investment is a loan that an SBIC provides to a business, and that loan must be paid back by the business, along with any interest that may have accrued. In exchange for financial assistance, a Small Business Investment Company (SBIC) typically receives equity in the company it invests in. There are occasions when a Small Business Investment Company will invest in a company through both finance and stock. A financial investment like this would consist of not just loans but also ownership shares. A typical investment made by an SBIC is spread out over a period of three years.

The Economic Opportunity Loans

Since the early 1960s, one of the components of the anti-poverty programs implemented in the United States has been the provision of subsidized loans to low-income adult borrowers. This is used in order to stimulate the ownership of small businesses by those individuals. The Economic Opportunity Act of 1964 gave President Lyndon B. Johnson the authority to create the Economic Opportunity Loan (EOL) program as part of his War on Poverty initiative. The United States Small Business Administration (SBA) provided EOL loans. These are presented as long-term loans, to disadvantaged enterprise owners, the majority of whom were minority-business borrowers. The qualifications for eligibility were previously taken to suggest that loans would only be made available to low-income individuals. However, this turned out not to be the case. Later on, the criteria for eligibility were broadened to include individuals who had been denied the opportunity to start a business on equal terms.

An extensive study was conducted between 1967 and 1970 on all EOL loans made to African Americans and nonminority whites. This study was made in order to assist individuals in New York City, Boston, and in Chicago in order to establish new small businesses. The study followed loan repayment up until November 1973. In total, 124 loans for finance entrance were available. Of these, 80 were given to black borrowers, while 40 were given to white borrowers. As of the end of November 1973, in accordance to the 124 loans, 46 of those loans were either up to date or had been repaid in full, 68 of them had been written off as being uncollectible, and 10 of them were behind on payments but were still considered active loans. The overall delinquent and default rate of 62.9 percent prompted the authors to make the suggestion that, if EOL loans were to be resumed, the SBA should establish trade-off functions. This trade off function would be between newly formed loans and failures. After suffering from high rates of loan default, the number of EOL loans actually began to decline rapidly after 1972, and the program was eventually terminated in 1984.

The EOL loan scheme failed in part due to an apparent contradiction. The borrowers who were successful in repaying their loans tended to come from higher income brackets. Although they were obviously qualified for the loans, a significant number of the truly poor receivers did not succeed. After the EOL program had helped its intended audience, there were not many successful ones were left standing. The poor success of the program can be attributed to the fact that the loan activities did not reach the targeted client demographic.

More recent, The SBA maintains offices in every state, employs more than 2,000 employees, and spends about $985 million annually. The agency helps 1 million entrepreneurs and small business owners annually. President Obama moved the SBA to his Cabinet in January 2012, a position it last held under Clinton.

Other Development Programs

Centers for the Development of Small Businesses

Funding for around 900 Small Business Development Center locations comes from a combination of contributions from state governments and the Small Business Administration. This is usually in the form of matching grants. Community colleges, state universities, and/or other institutions that foster entrepreneurial activity frequently house SBDCs, alongside one another.

Women's Business Centers

There are currently 110 Women's Business Centers across the country, many of which are situated in underserved but easily accessible areas. These centers are sponsored by providing matching funds to charitable groups. They frequently cater to home-based and other types of small businesses.

Service Corps of Retired Executives (SCORE)

The Small Business Administration (SBA) provides Service Corps of Retired Executives (SCORE) with funding on an annual basis. This is so that it can supervise about 350 chapters of volunteers, who offer free mentoring and counseling to business owners and entrepreneurs.

Chapter 5:
The Evaluation of Its Domestic & Public Interest

Initiatives in the 1960s

In the 1960s, the Small Business Administration (SBA) decided to pay more attention to other areas of domestic and public interest, such as poverty and minorities. The Small Business Administration (SBA) made the decision to support newly established companies that had been overlooked and were unable to attract financiers for help. This help was needed despite the fact that these companies were considered to be competent. Because of this, in 1964, the Equal Opportunity Loan program (EOL) was conceived and established. This initiative lowered the standards for obtaining credit and lowered the amount of collateral that was required from applicants who were judged to be living below the poverty threshold. Around this period, the Small Business Administration (SBA) started looking into the rate at which people were going into self-employment.

The data below is from the U.S. Bureau of Labor Statistics, TED. The illustration depicts The Economic Daily, Self - employment rates, 1948-2003, August 24, 2004 with the illustrated trend:

The percentage of people who were self-employed saw a significant decline from the 1940s through the 1960s. In 1948, it stood at 12 percent, but by 1970, it had dropped to 6.9 percent. Since the 1970s, the rate of people working for themselves has been relatively constant, at roughly 7 percent, with a margin of error of +/-0.5 percent. The rate stood at 6.5 percent in the year 2009.

Initiatives in 1970

In the 1970s, research developed into a significant tool that assisted the SBA, which was especially important given the presence of inflation at the time. The SBA was keeping an eye on and providing assistance in a wide variety of important sectors.

Both the transportation and energy sectors were of particular interest. Because of the consequences of the Arab oil embargo in 1973, it became possible to determine when the supply of retail gas dealers was in danger. As a result, the number of retail gas stations dropped by more than 20 percent. This was partly because of recently enacted restrictions that, for reasons of efficiency and fairness, gave newer retailers an advantage over more established ones. In a significant part of the transportation system, there was a requirement to concentrate attention as well. There was a reorganization of Northern Railroads and federal subsidies in relation to railway services as a result of Conrad and Amtrak's reorganization at the time. This meant that the Small Business Administration (SBA) had to come to the assistance of a large number of small enterprises that would be forced to make difficult decisions. This was due to the fact that many railway services were terminated. Congress was concerned about the conflict that arose between these two huge corporations and the smaller enterprises. In order to compete with large businesses, small businesses required a voice in the formation of public policy. Therefore, the Office of Advocacy was established within the SBA in the year 1976.

Older individuals were more likely to be Independent Contractors

People who work for themselves tended to be of retirement age, while younger people were far less likely to be self-employed. This has remained relatively stable over the course of several years.

Without exception, people tended to engage in self-employment more frequently as they get older.

From this 2002 illustration from the U. S. Census Bureau, an interesting pattern can be seen in the population of adults aged 65 and older in the below graph.

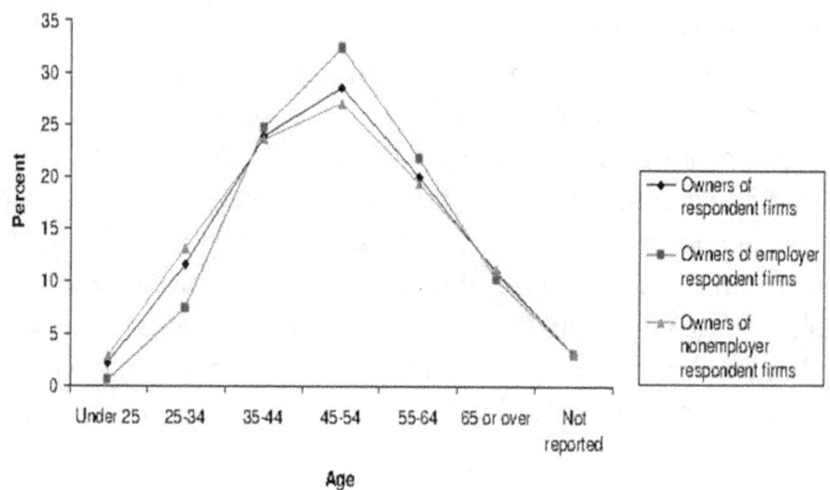

Source: U.S. Census Bureau, 2002 Survey of Business Owners
Characteristics of Business Owners – Released September 27, 2006

Furthermore, the percentage of adults aged 65 or older who were working for themselves fell from 19.5 percent in 1997 to 15.3 percent in 2003. In 1997, this percentage was 19.5 percent. Over the course of just a few years, there has been a considerable decline in the proportion of people in that age bracket who are self-employed. During the same time period, the percentage of people working for themselves fell across other age categories as well, albeit to a lesser extent.

Chapter 6:
Advocacy & Economic Trends

The SBA's primary objective was to complete trend research on small businesses, highlight the positive contributions these companies make to the economy, and work toward the passage of appropriate legislation. One of the most significant advantages offered by this part of the SBA is the fact that small companies are typically in the vanguard of innovation, not just in the United States but also in other countries. Economist have noted that small businesses are usually the key advocators of new ideas in most countries.

Office of Advocacy

The Office of Advocacy is charged by Congress with the responsibility of acting as an independent voice, inside the Federal Government, on behalf of the approximately 27.2 million small companies that are located all throughout the United States. The President, with the advice and consent of the Senate, appoints a Chief Counsel for Advocacy from the private sector to head the Office. This individual is responsible for representing the views, concerns, and interests of small businesses, formally, before Congress, the White House, and federal and state regulatory agencies.

The Regulatory Flexibility Act (RFA) requires federal agencies to evaluate the effect of their regulations. These evaluations are conducted on small businesses to consider alternatives that impose a lower level of burden on those businesses. The Office of Information and Regulatory Affairs (OIRA) monitors and reports annually on the compliance of federal agencies with the RFA.

Small entities include nonprofit organizations, governmental jurisdictions, and for-profit companies with less than 500 employees. The views of the OIRA are to be taken into consideration before any proposed regulations are implemented, and Executive Order 13272 mandates that the Office provide training to federal agencies on how to comply with RFA laws. The Office is one of the most important national sources of information on the current condition of small businesses. The OIRA's importance is also used to seek the factors that influence the development and expansion of small businesses. It conducts economic and statistical research into matters affecting the competitive strength of small businesses and jobs created by small businesses. In addition, it analyzes the impact of federal laws, regulations, and programs on small businesses, and it makes recommendations. These recommendations are presented to policymakers for appropriate adjustments to meet the special needs of small businesses.

In addition, regional advocates improve contact between the community of small businesses and the Chief Counsel. They help identify new issues and problems of small businesses by monitoring the effect of federal and state regulations and policies on the local business communities within their regions. In their role as the direct link between the Chief Counsel and local business owners, State and local government agencies, State legislatures, and small business organizations serve as the direct link between Chief Counsel and local business owners.

SBA advocates, available at *advocacy.sba.gov*, can assist with the following problems that small businesses face:

If you believe that new laws being considered by the government could have a negative impact on your company.

If you require information regarding the economy and small businesses.

Additionally, the Office of Advocacy acts as an independent representative for small businesses and brings their concerns to the attention of Congress, the White House, and other government agencies.

Economic Trends:

The mission of the Office of International Trade (OIT) is to foster an environment in which trade and international economic policies are favorable to small businesses. This is done by providing assistance to small businesses, in an effort to gain access to export markets and by participating in activities related to trade policy and international commercial affairs. This is relation to the actions carried out by the larger United States government entities. These operations, which include educational initiatives, programs, and services for technical support, risk management, and trade financing products, are aimed to facilitate both entry and growth into the international marketplace.

The Small Business Administration's (SBA) export promotion initiatives for small businesses include financial and technical help. Then these initiatives are delivered on a nationwide scale. The 7(a) program of the Small Business Administration (SBA) offers export financing products such as long-term, short-term, and revolving lines of credit. These products are managed by a team of field-based export specialists who are stationed in US Export Assistance Centers (USEACs). They work with the United States Department of Commerce as well as the Export-Import Bank of the United States. In addition, they collaborate closely with commercial lenders, Small Business Development Centers, and local business development organizations in order to maximize the effectiveness of their efforts.

A business that qualifies for the available financial assistance can get up to $1.25 million over a term of up to 25 years. This assistance can be used for the purchase of real estate and up to 15 years term time for the purchase of equipment.

Loans from programs that provide working capital typically offer renewable financing for a period of 12 months. SBA Export Express provides a streamlined and speedy approval process for loan amounts of up to $250,000. This is to enterprises that require financing for smaller quantities usually.

Technical assistance includes making export training and legal assistance available to current and potential small business exporters. This means collaborating with the thirty Small Business Development Centers across the country that specialize in international trade and the United States Trade Information Center, run by the federal government.

The Small Business Administration is obligated to collaborate with other government agencies involved in international trade. This is done in order to fulfill its responsibility of ensuring that the interests of small businesses are effectively represented. This means both bilateral and multilateral trade discussions can be made. The Organization for Economic Cooperation and Development and the Asia-Pacific Economic Cooperation are both formal multilateral organizations. These are supported by the United States Government in areas that are concerned with small businesses as well. OIT represents both the SBA and the government in both organizations. The participation of the SBA in the formation of trade policy is coordinated with the Office of the United States Trade Representative and the International Trade Administration of the Department of Commerce. Participation in the small business industry sector advisory group on international trade is one way for members of the private sector to provide feedback. This gives the members the chance to speak on matters pertaining to trade policy. In addition, OIT provides assistance to the most important trade initiatives undertaken by the federal government, including the Trade Promotion Authority, the Central American Free Trade Area, and the Free Trade Area of the Americas. The Departments of Commerce and State, as well as the Agency for International Development and the United States Trade Representatives, look to the Small Business Administration (SBA) to share ideas. The above also look to the SBA to supply certain countries with the technical skills needed by small businesses.

The OIT in Washington, DC, is responsible for coordinating the participation and operation of USEACs on behalf of the SBA, including a budget, policy, and administrative matters. It is involved in a number of different interagency trade and financial programs and initiatives. The Office of International Trade (OIT) provides representations on trade and international economic policy to the cabinet-level Trade Promotion Coordinating Committee. In addition to this, it is involved in the Industry Sector Advisory Council on Small Business International Trade, as well as the Task Force on Small Business International Trade that is funded by Congress.

HUBZone Program:

The HUBZone program offers assistance in obtaining federal contracts to small businesses. Small businesses must meet certain criteria and must be located in historically underutilized business zones. The goal of the program is to boost employment, capital investment, and economic growth in these regions, which may include Indian reservations. The Office works in coordination with other federal agencies and the municipal governments of local communities to maximize the use of available resources. This is in order to provide assistance to qualified small enterprises that are situated in HUBZone zones. The program sets goals for the number of awards that are intended to be given to HUBZone small businesses and provides for set-asides, sole source awards, and price evaluation preferences for those enterprises.

For further information regarding the 8(a) Business Development Program, please contact the Office of Business Development. The Office offers help to small enterprises by facilitating their access to loans and contracts, as well as cash and credit. Additionally, the Office offers business counseling, training courses, and technical guidance.

Concerning the Native Americans, the Office of Native American Affairs was established to assist and encourage the creation, development, and expansion of Native American-owned small businesses. This is accomplished by the Office of Native American Affairs. The Office of Native American Affairs develops and implements initiatives that are designed to address the challenges that Native Americans face. This is in specific to their efforts to start, develop, and expand small businesses most of all. Additionally, in an effort to address the one-of-a-kind circumstances that are faced by business owners that operate off of reservations, the Office addressed process of developing a web-based resource. This was to be known as the "Tribal Self-Assessment Tool." Its purpose is to make it possible for tribal countries to evaluate their vision and aspirations, in light of their existing governing structures, cultures, capabilities, and resources. The application should downloaded for free from the internet when it accessible.

Chapter 7:
Legal and Justice Assistance

In spite of the fact that the above organizations were helpful for the lobbying needs of "small firms," at the beginning of the 1980s, there emerged a new problem that affected small enterprises on an individual basis. During the course of the case, a number of smaller businesses started incurring losses that were beginning to be rather large. This was not because fees were awarded to the opposing side; rather, it was because fees were awarded to their own attorneys. The problem was related to legal issues. It was common for attorneys to charge exorbitant fees, which were such a financial strain for their clients that it dissuaded some people from seeking legal assistance at all. Because of this issue, the Equal Access to Justice Act, also known as the EAJA, was passed into law in the year 1980. The government was able to recover legal fees with the assistance of the EAJA. Additionally, it was helpful in supporting small enterprises in complying with any legal regulations.

Litigation

Affirmative and defensive litigation, including the liquidation and litigation of Small Business Investment Companies (SBICs), as well as precedent-setting debt collection litigation, are handled by this division in federal court. Additionally, the Department serves as the Agency's Freedom of Information Act (FOIA) legal counsel. Regarding 8(a) suspensions and terminations, as well as suspensions and debarments involving SBA financial programs, when it comes before the Office of Hearings and Appeals. In addition to cases involving legal challenges in environmental, employment, bankruptcy, commercial, procurement, administrative, tort, and creditor rights, its practice areas include constitutional law and regulatory enforcement.

Financial Regulation and Lender Control

The Office of General Council, also known as OGC's EAJA team offers legal guidance and support to program offices in charge of secondary market transactions. It also is in charge of small company investment firms, disaster loans, surety bond guarantees, and guaranteed business loans. This division provides legal assessment and clearance for various financial transactions involving program participants. In addition, it aids the program offices in the creation of regulations and comments on new legislation also.

Basic Law (Labor and Employment)

This team represents the agency as legal counsel in labor and employment law disputes before the Federal Labor Relations Authority, the Equal Employment Opportunity Commission, the Merit Systems Protection Board, and the SBA's Office of Hearings and Appeals. This division participates in local and national labor negotiations and provides advice to the agency on matters relating to employee conduct and performance.

Contract Law

The OGC offers legal advice on federal procurement rules and laws that apply to small enterprises. This section specifically provides guidance to SBA program offices regarding all facets of the agency's numerous small business government contracting. It assists with input on business development programs. These can include the size standards program, for Servicing Disabled Veteran Owned (SDVO) Small Business set aside programs, the 8(a) Business Development Program, and the HUBZone program.

Regarding Agency contracts and grant awards, this OGC also offers program authorities legal counsel and assistance. In addition to drafting and interpreting small business procurement regulations, the attorneys in this group represent the agency in administrative litigation involving procurement. It also assists in handling protests regarding the eligibility of HUBZone, 8(a), and SDVO small businesses, and counsels Agency officials on how to identify and engage in competitive sourcing. This may be for activities that are not inherently governmental as well.

Field Activities

Regarding all programs run by the Regional and District Offices, this division offers legal counsel and support to Agency representatives in Washington and the field. The group specifically provides advice and examines the actions taken by SBA field offices with regard to the agency's program, including the 504 Loan Program, the 8(a) Business Development Program, and the 7(a) Loan Program. This team aids the Office of Litigation and the US Attorney's Office when the agency is a party to litigation and offers ethics guidance to regional and district officials.

Legislation and Budgeting

All SBA offices receive legal advice and direction from this group on a variety of legal matters. This includes issues involving the budget, appropriations, legislation, Congressional activities, regulations, reports, Office of Management and Budget (OMB) guidance and procedures. In addition, this also includes information collected under the Paperwork Reduction Act, and financial and performance reporting mandated by the Government Performance and Results Act, as amended. Furthermore, this group organizes Office of General Council (OGC) responses to legislative and regulatory referrals from OMB, Congressional testimony, agency replies to Congressional inquiries, and other related issues.

Outreach

This team offers field offices and the agency's headquarters legal counsel on sponsorships, gifts to the organization, memorandums of understanding, and social media. Additionally, this group offers the Agency advice on a range of topics, such as advisory committees, intellectual property, and logo usage.

Ethics

The Designated Agency Ethics Official (DAEO) and the Alternate DAEO are chosen by the Administrator to manage, coordinate, and oversee the Agency's Ethics Program. They both work out of the Office of General Counsel. This section controls the agency's financial disclosure reporting procedure, offers guidance on limitations on employees' engagement in partisan political activities, and offers immunizing ethics counsel and training. Additionally, this group offers guidance and makes decisions regarding the agency's employee conduct policies, limitations on the provision of SBA funding, GSA gift-travel requirements, and OPM guidelines for the Combined Federal Campaign.

Export Legal Assistance Network (ELAN)

The Export Legal Assistance Network (ELAN), sponsored by the Federal Bar Association in partnership with the US Department of Commerce and the Small Business Administration, is a group of knowledgeable international trade attorneys who volunteer their time to offer initial legal consultations to people and companies who are new exporters or importers and/or who are looking for legal advice on international trade issues. In addition, ELAN offers updates on official operations affecting international trade as well as links to US government resources.

Chapter 8:
Politics and Agency Regulation

Along with this, in the 1980s, the Regulatory Flexibility Act was created, which requested that government agencies evaluate what would occur if a certain regulation was placed on a small firm. This was done in conjunction with the previous point. This marked the beginning of a trend that recognizes enterprises in relation to their compliance with regulatory requirements and the potential implications of such requirements. During the Reagan administration, this issue received a significant amount of attention. For instance, in 1981, President Ronald Reagan issued an executive order that requested the Office of Management and Budget examine every new rule that was being proposed in order to determine what the most likely impact of that rule's costs and benefits would be on businesses of all sizes. This order was issued in response to a request made by Reagan. Finding ways to lessen the restrictions placed on firms was one of the strategies utilized in the deregulation movement. During the entire decade of the 1980s and during the first forty months of Ronald Reagan's presidency, he published 33,364 rules, the majority of which were related to deregulation. Deregulation was an area of policy favor that was the focus of all business until its abrupt halting. This was marked by the well-known savings and loan tragedy.

Attorneys for SBA Matters

You are probably aware that the Small Business Administration (SBA) of the United States of America keeps a comprehensive list of standards for lenders that issue SBA loans. One is under a legal obligation to comply with these regulations if one is a lender to small businesses. If one dose not, one run the risk of losing the guarantee on one's loans, as well as the ability to offer loans that are backed by the Small Business Administration (SBA). One can seek counsel from an outside attorney that specializes in SBA related law if one has a disagreement with the SBA.

Maintain a level of awareness of the most recent changes to SBA law and regulations, as well as any updates to small business lending policy. Ensure continued compliance with the SBA's current lending policies. Find your way through the tangled web of SBA legislation and government requirements. Deal with any concerns that may arise about the repayment, repair, or refusal of an SBA guarantee. Improve the quality of service you provide to your customers.

Agency Regulations

SBA regulations are backed by years of expertise while working with the SBA, as well as a staff of SBA attorneys who are aware lending laws. Include assistance in establishing or securing SBA lending authority as a Non-Federally Regulated Lender (NFRL) or a Small Business Lending Company (SBLC). Their service can be there in every step of the process, from application to repayment. The SBA offers proper loan structure and purchases backed by an SBA loan guarantee.

SBA loan portfolio audits can help with restructuring. SBA loans can be restructured, and SBA loans can also be foreclosed.

Chapter 9:
Fairness in Business

At the beginning of the 1990s, the emphasis was still on providing firms with a certain amount of political and statistical clout. Savings and loan institutions, however, were not the major target this time. The public's involvement, justice through small company participation in the creation of regulations, and lowering regulatory running costs were all given emphasis. Curtailing business regulation was, in fact, the trend, as evidenced by initiatives like President Clinton's Executive Order #12866, which involved the public and small businesses, and the Small Business Regulatory Enforcement Fairness Act of 1996. This established Congressional reviews, plain language criteria, and the establishment of a National Ombudsman to assist in regulator criticism.

As a part of the Small Business Regulatory Enforcement Fairness Act, which was passed by Congress in 1996, the national ombudsman and 10 Regulatory Fairness Boards were both established at that time (SBREFA).

Small businesses, small government entities, and small nonprofit organizations are protected under the Small Business Regulatory Enforcement Fairness Act, thanks to Section 222 of SBREFA.

There is now a way for the 509 organizations that have been subjected to unjust regulatory enforcement actions by federal agencies to register their comments regarding these actions. The comments and concerns of small businesses can be submitted via email, fax, regular mail, or by testifying in person at one of the many ombudsman hearings that take place all over the country.

The role of the ombudsman is to act as a neutral liaison between the concerns of small businesses and the affected agencies so that comments can be included in the report. Each of the Regulatory Fairness Boards, also known as RegFair, is comprised of five volunteer members who are the owners, operators, or officers of small business concerns. These members are appointed to three-year terms by the Administrator of the Small Business Administration. Each RegFair Board is required to hold at least one meeting per year with the ombudsman to discuss issues that are important to small businesses in relation to the enforcement or compliance activities of federal agencies. They are also to report to the ombudsman on substantiated instances of excessive enforcement, and provide comment on the annual report to Congress prior to its publication.

Chapter 10:
Politics and Regulation Flexibility Focus

Congress made the decision to improve the Regulatory Flexibility Act of 1980 in March 1996. In addition, it encouraged the SBA's Administrators to work with the Ombudsman for Small Business and Agriculture Regulatory Enforcement. They required federal agencies to develop policies that lowered or waived civil penalties for small enterprises. The Ombudsmen were expected to provide reports on regulatory compliance, enforcement, views, and small company owner complaints.

Introduction

When rules have a significant economic impact on a significant number of small entities, agencies are required by the Regulatory Flexibility Act (RFA) to take into account how their rules will affect small entities and to evaluate alternatives. Through these alternatives they would have a chance at achieving the goals of the rule without unduly burdening small entities. Congress's intention to lower obstacles to competition and encourage agencies to think about methods to adapt rules to the size of the regulated firms is inherent in the RFA.

If there are significant legal, policy, factual, or other reasons why a rule will have an impact on small firms, the RFA does not require agencies to necessarily minimize that impact. The RFA simply demands that agencies establish, to the extent practicableness. They are hoping for practical economic impact of the rule on small entities. They would like investigative regulatory alternatives for minimizing any major economic impact on a considerable number of such firms, and justify their regulatory decisions. A requirement of Executive Order 13272, which was signed on August 13, 2002, is that agencies create policies and procedures to encourage adherence to the RFA. Therefore, every time the EEOC starts their regulatory process, the following procedures—which are based on advice provided by the Office of Advocacy at the Small Business Administration (SBA) should be followed.

Initial Analysis of Regulatory Flexibility

The RFA mandates the creation of an initial regulatory flexibility analysis (IRFA) if the EEOC is unable to certify that a regulation won't have a major impact on a large number of small businesses. The IRFA needs to be made available for public review and comment. In addition, the IRFA or a synopsis of it needs to be published in the Federal Register with the notice of proposed rulemaking. According to the RFA, agencies must make sure that small entities have a chance to participate in any rulemaking that will affect them. The statute recommends strategies such as including a warning that the proposed rule may have a significant impact on small entities in any advance Notice of Proposed Rulemaking, (NPRM). The statute recommends disseminating information about NPRMs to publications that small entities are likely to obtain, contacting interested small entities directly. The statute recommends holding conferences or public hearings about the rule for small entities. Also, the SBA Chief Counsel for Advocacy must receive the IRFA.

The IRFA must: (1) outline the proposed rule's effects on small entities; and (2) outline any alternatives that will lessen the effects, while achieving the stated goals of the relevant statutes. An IRFA must include the following details when outlining how the proposed regulation will affect small businesses/entities. They are:

- An overview of the factors that led to the Equal Employment Opportunity Commission considering taking action.
- A condensed explanation of the proposed rule's goals in addition to its rationale from a legal standpoint.
- A description as well as, if at all possible, an estimation of the total number of small entities to which the proposed rule will apply.
- A description of the anticipated reporting, recordkeeping, and other requirements for compliance with the proposed rule. This should include an estimate of the classes of small organizations that will be subject to the requirement, as well as the long-term and short-term compliance costs should be available.
- An inventory, to the extent that it is possible, of all applicable federal regulations that could be considered redundant, redundantly covered, or in conflict with the proposed rule should be available as well.

The Office of Advocacy at the Small Business Administration recommends to government agencies that, when formulating and analyzing regulatory alternatives, they should do so at the earliest possible stage of the rulemaking process. The Office of Advocacy at the Small Business Administration recommends agencies consult with small entities, as well as consider and evaluate the relative benefits of the rule to large and small entities. The RFA specifies that agency analyses must include a discussion of alternatives. This may include the following:

- Establishing different compliance or reporting requirements for small entities.

- Clarifying or simplifying compliance or reporting requirements for small entities.
- Exempting certain or all small entities from all or part of the rule, or establishing different compliance or reporting requirements for large entities.

Final Regulatory Flexibility Analysis

The comments that were made on the proposed rule will be analyzed, and the results of that analysis will assist in determining whether or not the final rule will have a major impact on a considerable number of small organizations. In the event that there will be a major impact, a final regulatory flexibility analysis (FRFA) needs to be developed and submitted for publication in the Federal Register alongside the final rule. If there will not be an impact that is considered to be significant, a certification may be published alongside the final rule, along with the factual basis. Rulemakings cannot proceed directly from a certified proposed rule to a final rule that contains an FRFA without going through at least one intermediate step.

Although the requirements for an FRFA are considerably different than those for an IRFA, the need for agencies to evaluate the impact of the rule on small businesses and analyze regulatory alternatives, continues to be the primary focus. The following are the requirements, as outlined in the RFA:

- A condensed explanation of the reasons why the regulation was created and what its goals are.
- A summary of the main concerns presented by the public comments in response to the IRFA. Therefore, a summary of the assessment that the agency made of such issues,

and a statement of any changes that were made in the proposed rule, as a result of the comments should be given.

- A description of the tiny entities to which the regulation will apply, together with an estimate of the number of those small entities. In addition, there should be an explanation of why such an estimate is not available.

- A description of the anticipated reporting, recordkeeping, and other requirements for compliance with the rule should be available. Also, an estimate of the classes of small entities that will be subject to the requirement and the costs associated with compliance should be available.

- A description of the steps that the agency has taken to minimize the significant economic impact on small entities, including a statement of the factual, policy, and legal reasons for selecting the alternative adopted in the final rule should be available. This should also include an explanation of why each of the other significant alternatives to the rule that were considered by the agency was rejected by the agency.

As long as the RFA's requirements are satisfied, the RFA allows for agencies to create IRFAs and FRFAs in conjunction with or as a part of other mandatory analyses. This is allowed as long as the RFA's standards are met. For significant rules that are required to have a regulatory impact analysis prepared, in accordance with Executive Order 12866, for instance, agencies may choose to prepare both analyses at the same time.

Chapter 11:
Reducing Regulation Cost for Business

According to the Office of Advocacy in the Small Business Administration (SBA), one of the positive outcomes of policies that advocated for the reduction of regulatory action was that small businesses were able to realize savings of approximately $20.6 billion in reduced regulatory costs over the course of the years 1998, 1999, and 2000. This investigation revealed some unfavorable information, such as the fact that the cost of complying with regulatory policy in the United States was $750 billion in the year 1999. Even though there have been these largely political factors involving regulatory pluses and minuses, there are still grassroots direct policies that can help key businesses such as transportation and agricultural production. For instance, in the year 2000, the Office of Science and Technology at the Environmental Protection Agency (EPA) was able to save small company owners $100 million by just modifying two different regulations. One of these regulations pertained to metal items, while the other addressed the cleaning of transportation equipment. In addition, the Center for Food Safety and Applied Nutrition within the Department of Health and Human Services completely revamped its decision-making process. As a result, it is now working directly with the Small Business Administration and proprietors of small businesses to formulate food manufacturing policy.

How the SBA Helps Small Businesses Get Loans

The United States Small Business Administration (SBA) facilitates the acquisition of finance for small enterprises by establishing criteria for loans and minimizing the risk and costs incurred by lenders. These loans guaranteed by the SBA make it simpler for small enterprises to acquire the capital that they want.

The Advantages of Obtaining Loans Guaranteed By the SBA

Loans guaranteed by the Small Business Administration (SBA) typically have interest rates and costs that are competitive with those of non-guaranteed loans. Some loans come with ongoing support in the form of counseling and education that can assist you in the launch and operation of your business. Unique advantages include lower initial deposits, flexible requirements for overhead costs, and, for some loans, no need to put up security.

Stay safe

By being vigilant and watching out for warning indicators, you may protect yourself from unscrupulous lenders. Some creditors subject borrowers to terms that are unethical and abusive by employing tactics like fraud and coercion. Be wary of interest rates that are noticeably higher than the rates offered by competitors, as well as fees that account for more than 5 percent of the total value of the loan. Make it a point to verify that the lending institution provides the annual percentage rate as well as the complete payment plan. It is unacceptable for a lender to request that you make false statements on documents or leave blank signature fields. Avoid giving in to the pressure to take out a loan. Before you sign for your next loan, it is in your best interest to investigate the other offers on the market and to consider consulting a financial planner, an accountant, or an attorney.

Chapter 12:
SBA Technology Change

Most recently, the SBA's primary areas of operation and attention have shifted even further in their configuration. The SBA is being compelled to adapt as a result of a technological imperative. It has made efforts to become more intuitive and derive technology that is easier to use. And finally, in order to ensure its own and the small business's survival, it has been forced to compete and struggle.

This has been similar to the steps taken by many other organizations to keep up with technological demands in terms of structural changes. According to an article that was published in the *American Banker* in the year 2000, the Small Business Administration (SBA) had begun testing web-based solutions in order to make the processing of loans both quicker and more cost-effective. According to the information presented in the article, the new transmission mechanism of lending activity may be simplified in the near future. There would also be a huge reduction in the amount of paperwork and handling involved. This would be a significant reduction in the amount of paper used by the SBA, whose portfolio has tripled in size since 1990. Together with the National Community Reinvestment Coalition, the Small Business Administration was using the technology of this kind in their collaboration. Through their efforts, this group brings together borrowers and lenders. Since the beginning of this community express initiative in 1999, a total of over $11 million worth of loans have been distributed. Their focus on technological helps extend even farther, the Office of the National Ombudsman for the Small

Business Administration in the creation of a website that welcomes feedback from visitors.

The American economy relies heavily on its vast number of small companies. The spirit of enterprise is crucial to the achievement of the American Dream. The idea that one may build a successful life from nothing is enticing. The idea that you can achieve your goals with nothing more than your brains, your perseverance, and your own hard work is almost romantic.

Small firms and entrepreneurs may, thank goodness, count on technology to make their lives easier. This assists them in achieving their own personal version of the American Dream. Since the general public gained access to the internet in the early nineties, a slide toward more innovation has been underway even more.

Guiding Principles

Always Put the Customer First

The Small Business Administration (SBA) is dedicated to putting its customers' needs first by enhancing the customer experience (CX). This begins on the first day of small business contact with the agency and continuing through the final day. The 21st Century Integrated Digital Experience Act (IDEA) mandates the utilization of qualitative and quantitative data collected from all areas of the agency. This utilization is to enhance the experience of the agency's customers, and to provide a method for determining which aspects of the experience can be improved. As a result of these efforts, the agency will be able to comprehend the voice and needs the client. With input it the SBA will all be able to enhance the services offered to the small businesses of the United States and fulfill the purpose of their agency even more. By improving core services, the Small Business Administration personnel will be able to maintain 100 percent of their concentration on addressing the requirements of their clients. Thus, better information will help the employee experience be improved also.

Create an Innovative, Digital Enterprise

The Small Business Administration (SBA) kicked off the process of transforming itself into an innovative and digital organization by utilizing technology that gave it the ability to harness the power of the cloud years ago. This digital transformation began with a focus on high-impact, customer services, and focus that has not changed.

This is done to better position the SBA to accomplish its core mission, which is to provide relevant content and services on topics such as access to capital, counseling, federal contracting, disaster assistance, and entrepreneurial education. It is of the utmost importance that the SBA makes use of its business transformation goal that it has envisioned to accomplish its objectives as well. Only after that will the SBA be able to develop a digital enterprise that is efficient, centered on the client, and aligned with the businesses it serves.

Help Complete a Mission: A Capable and Ready I.T. Workforce

In order to provide assistance to America's small businesses, the Small Business Administration (SBA) needs to plan for and adapt to the ongoing changes in technology, safeguard data, and make better use of technologies to enhance the customer experience. In order to accomplish this goal, the SBA will need a sufficient number of people, as well as the necessary resources, and applied knowledge to get the job done well. In addition to this, it is necessary to have adequate performance assessment criteria. This should be coupled with accountability as well, in place so that the agency's mission goals and objectives may be attained properly.

Govern Information Technology to Better Serve Small Businesses

In order to fully realize the promise of information technology, choices on strategy, priorities, and what gets funded, through accurate information need to be firmly rooted in the operations of the SBA, only then will the benefit of technology be complete. Keeping in mind that the resources available to the SBA are limited, the major concern that needs to be addressed when determining information technology priorities is the question of how to effectively serve the nation's small businesses.

Improve Position Regarding Cyber Security

By implementing robust cyber security and privacy programs, those at the SBA are able to safeguard the confidential information that has been entrusted to them.

The following are some of the most important components of an efficient cyber security program:

- Identifying and comprehending threats to the mission.
- Defending information systems and operational technology against cyberattacks
- Repairing damage caused by attacks
- Preventing further attacks from occurring

These are all part of the process. It is crucial for the well-being of the Small Business Administration as well as its customers and stakeholders to create and maintain a successful cybersecurity program, which needs coordination throughout the agency, adequate resources, and careful management.

65

Chapter 13:
User Friendliness and Attention to Minorities

Another area of importance, the desire to be seen as user-friendly is a quality present in this sector of public service as well. In this mind set, as part of the SBA's initiatives to draw attention to African American and Hispanic small enterprises in relation to their micro solicitation. In Indiana, minority-owned small businesses like barbershops were visited by U. S. SBA representatives in the year 2000 to learn from their business methods.

According to the SBA, the proposed revisions would simplify the requirements for small business owners and reinstate eligibility for over 20,000 companies. This was important, because many of these small businesses had lost status due to the effects of inflation.

Transparency: SBA makes an effort to make statistics and other information about agency programs and activities accessible to clients and stakeholders. Greater accountability, accessibility, and responsiveness will be made possible with greater transparency.

Involvement: SBA works to boost participation by utilizing novel methods and techniques to solicit suggestions and criticism from the general public. Public participation is used to increase the SBA's efficiency and raise the standard of its workers' judgments.

The collaboration between SBA and all partners will hopefully create better outcomes. By doing this, the SBA will improve participation from interested parties in government activity, particularly with small companies.

Business.gov Metrics Dashboard

To gain insight into the requirements and preferences of small business owners that visit Business.gov, now called SBA.gov, the dashboard offers online analytics data gathered from various tracking methods. This SBA page always improving offers new tools and resources the agency offers to assist the nation's small companies in starting, expanding, and managing their operations as determined by data submitted by SBA.gov users. Each quarter, the dashboard is updated. Metrics data is made available to the public because it demonstrates how the agency gathers and utilizes information about site visitors and reveals how well the website performs, as indicated by user satisfaction comments. For years, the SBA web team has gathered and evaluated this data for internal use. The data is made available via the dashboard since it poses no concerns to security or privacy. For the agency, metrics data is a valuable source of feedback. Web analytics can help the SBA agency identify priority content or information that requires upgrading in order to make websites more user-friendly. Web metrics that are made available to the public give consumers vital information about the small business community as well as a better understanding of the site's internal operations. The SBA intended to put in place a comparable dashboard for SBA.gov, the agency's primary website, based on the success of the Business.gov Metrics Dashboard. This ever improving task was done through the Flagship Initiative, which was there to make SBA.gov have a better start and continue into the future.

Customer Relationship Management Tool

To help headquarters and field operations staff in giving borrowers, lenders, partners, and stakeholders a customer-focused response, SBA is introducing a Customer Relationship

Management (CRM) Tool. This toll was an important tool in the goal specified in the Recovery Act. The CRM Tool, which was used for enhancing, streamlining, and automating data relevant to loan processing and lender oversight, now improved even more.

With it, employees may access information faster and in a clearer format thanks to the CRM Tool, which compiles data from many platforms. Dashboards and ad hoc reports are essential for the presentation of the data. Additionally, it is possible to organize and monitor communications with important stakeholders centrally. These skills will increase the SBA's ability to respond to FOIA requests and information requests from Congress in a timely and efficient manner. The CRM Tool's initial release was and has been distributed throughout the organization. Additional improvements were and are planned to coordinate communication and interaction with the public, create better mapping tools, and integrate current applications.

Assistance to Minorities and Women

The SBA is dedicated to assisting women and underrepresented groups in growing their business participation also. It provides microloans, a program for minority-owned small businesses, and the dissemination of educational resources in Spanish. By giving regional offices more decision-making power it has sought to improved its responsiveness to small companies. This includes the use of developing high-tech instruments for grant and loan transactions, as well for eligibility reviews too.

Chapter 14:
Mistrust and Building Trust with the Public

A report estimates that 8,400 companies were owned by people of color. Mistrust by people of color was one of the issues the SBA representatives ran across in the agency's efforts to serve everyone. They targeted residents in communities where there was little faith in governmental authority in an effort to change that.

SBA Subsidy Programs Problems:

Ten complaints were raised against the SBA and its support programs:

1. Some people gained from SBA subsidies at the expense of many others. The SBA's flagship 7(a) subsidized loan programs, which accounted for more than 90 percent of all non-disaster SBA loan guarantees, actually representing slightly more than 1 percent of all small company loans outstanding at one time, according to a GAO analysis.

2. Restaurants, gas stations, beauty parlors, and dental offices are the sectors that gain the most from SBA subsidies. Furthermore, the companies who obtained SBA backed loans made up a very small portion of all the businesses operating in those sectors. Why did the federal government have a duty to favor a select few businesses like these markets?

3. When a pizzeria received support from the federal government, and it indicated that rival pizzerias that did not receive any subsidies and had suffered, this indicated those in other businesses who were looking for funding were also at a disadvantage. This appeared to be so because they were either

missing out on opportunities or had to accept less advantageous conditions. The SBA used this data to review for improvement.

4. Politics and subsidies are closely related. An SBA rule forbid lenders from using SBA backed loans to fund marijuana-related enterprises at one time. At the same time, a Massachusetts brewery that the SBA supported was celebrating. A Mexico styled winery, the breweries and marijuana companies needed better made regulations for them. Commercial activity often becomes politicized as a result of bad planning of subsidies distribution at times. Finding balance through proper review must be sought always.

5. The subsidies, according to SBA supporters, are required to address market failure in commercial lending. Often that maybe because there is an information gap between lenders and borrowers. Also, lenders may be unable to meet the funding needs of otherwise deserving small entity companies. These claims have been presented by advances like credit scoring and the development of lending relationships between creditors and borrowers. In addition to the above, the use and the significant impact that personal savings, assets, and credit cards were shown to impact small businesses as well.

6. Supporters of the SBA also contended that the agency's loans encouraged financial institutions to provide loans to companies who are unable to secure credit elsewhere. The definition of credit elsewhere according to pertinent federal statutes may have been the availability of credit from non-Federal sources on fair terms and conditions. The GAO's discovering that companies who received SBA backed loans might have gotten non-subsidized financing was not entirely unexpected. It's important to note that there are instances when loans just shouldn't be made as well.

Nevertheless, financial markets, not political markets, maybe should decide when this is the case most of all. In fact, the high default rates on SBA-backed loans demonstrated how frequently the government's involvement in the credit market misallocating capital for useless purposes occurred to often.

7. It was and is uncommon to find a politician who doesn't use the creation of jobs as a justification for a government program. However, as an article by the Congressional Research Service on the SBA and job creation explains, Economists frequently do not consider job creation as a reason for providing federal support to small companies. They contend that over time, such support is more likely to reallocate employment money within the economy than to create a new set of jobs. Sadly, the press releases from the SBA and from news sources are what the public sees. The bigger, more widespread economic losses brought on by these market-distorting subsidies aren't as easily visible or, reported on.

8. The banking sector opposed the SBA's creation in 1953, but they changed their minds after the SBA shifted from direct lending to insuring loans made by other lenders. The explanation is straightforward. When an SBA backed loan defaults, the Bank is compensated for up to 85 percent of the loan balance. Therefore, SBA guaranteed loans are generally risk-free for banks and extremely profitable if there is a loan loss.

9. It could be argued that SBA loan guarantees are a type of business-like welfare for big banks. Major financial institutions, including Wells Fargo, JP Morgan Chase, and others were, at a time, among the top-ranking SBA backed lenders.

10. A larger company may have ended up benefiting from an SBA backed loan, even though it was formally made into a smaller business. The Office of the Inspector General of the SBA

discovered in March 2018 that $1.8 billion in SBA backed loans given to chicken farmers were probably improper since the farmers were essentially affiliates of significant poultry processors. However, this example demonstrated how subsidy schemes can be maneuvered to the benefit of unintended beneficiaries at times. To reiterate, maybe the federal government should work harder at finding more just methods for lending.

Solution: National City Bank

This was addressed by initiatives like the National City Bank that aimed to widen loan availability in relation to the SBA and loans. This Bank had introduced a $35,000 small business loan that was viewed as uncertain. This type of loan was available without security. For this set of potential customers, there is some optimism. The National Federation of Independent Businesses reported that its July index indicator increased by eight tenths in August 2000.

National City Bank, Cleveland's oldest Bank, in 2008, was acquired by Pittsburgh National Corporation and Provident National Corporation, which merged in 1983, now known as PNC, and was renowned for its business leadership, customer service, and community efforts. National City Corporation Bank (PNC) would safeguard the records that chronicled National City's history in addition to upholding the city's fundamental principles. National City kept an archive of its transactions and corporate connections, but notably of its consumer outreach in northern Ohio. These assets were supplemented by the holdings of a number of local archives, creating a comprehensive account of not only National City's history but also that of its forebears. The PNC Legacy Project is pleased to present the next fifteen items in the hopes that they may deepen visitors' respect and comprehension of earlier times.

The Bank then would be in a position to offer credit, lend money to the government, safeguard its deposits, provide Americans with a unified currency, and encourage trade and industry. It essentially assisted in putting the United States on an equal financial footing with the countries of Europe when combined with Alexander Hamilton's other financial initiatives at the time. It is known for doing the first mortgage in America. National City Corporation Bank also ended business in relation to risk management issues sighted by regulators.

Chapter 15:
SBA Still Finds Support

The SBA has collaborated on projects like the United States Regulatory Fairness Board Roundtable, which has a wider scope. The March 29, 2001, meeting of this board was centered on the requirements of small businesses. In addition to inviting individuals and businesses, this type of meeting was distinctive in that it included representatives from other regulatory bodies like the IRS, the Department of Labor, the EPA, and the Department of Agriculture. This forum's specific purpose was to collect suggestions for forming policies and, if necessary, restructuring. According to the 1996 Small Business Regulatory Enforcement Act, this endeavor was legal. With justice, this Act offered expression to the opinions of small businesses.

Regulatory Fairness Boards

Ten Regional Regulatory Fairness Boards for small businesses must be appointed by the SBA's Administrator. Five small company owners give of their time to make up the boards. The Regulatory Fairness Boards offer the Ombudsman advice on issues involving federal regulations that small businesses should be aware of. The National Ombudsman's Office's resources are made available to small businesses through the Regulatory Fairness Boards, whose actions are coordinated by the ombudsman.

John Kerry's Relief Package

Small enterprises in the Gulf Region could also take advantage of the assistance packages. This included:

- Quick approval of short-term loans or grants to enable businesses that are awaiting SBA loan approval to start rebuilding right away.
- Deferral of interest and payments on SBA catastrophe loans for a year.
- Access to 40 percent of the subcontracting budget used for the recovery and relief effort and 30 percent of all federal contracts.
- Historically Underutilized Business Zone (HUBZone) classification has been expanded, giving local small firms precedence when competing for government contracts.
- Increased business counseling and support offered by SBA entrepreneurial development centers, such as Small Business Development Centers, SCORE, Microloan Technical Assistance, Women's Business Centers, and Veterans Business Outreach Centers.
- More chances for small construction businesses to acquire SBA bonding assistance, which functions as a kind of contract insurance against financial loss.
- The availability of low-interest disaster loans for refinancing current disaster loans as well as current corporate debt.

Senators Kerry and Landrieu introduced the initially small company aid package as an amendment to the Commerce, Justice, and Science Appropriations Bill (S.2862), which was before the Senate.

The Bush Administration

At the 2008 Small Business Summit on April 18, President Bush met with representatives of small firms to discuss the administration's initiatives to support their competitiveness. Short-term economic uncertainty had been addressed by the federal government, while long-term economic uncertainty continued to affect small businesses and workers. There were some problems that were completely within their hands to fix, even though some of these sources of uncertainty were out of anyone's control. The President outlined actions Congress may have taken, particularly in the areas of tax and trade, to support the expansion of America's small companies.

The administration wanted to prioritize reducing tax uncertainty and increase trade as its top priority.

According to the Bush administration, by enacting free trade agreements with three democratic allies—Colombia, Panama, and South Korea—Congress had the chance to increase access to important export markets. It appeared that lawmakers on Capitol Hill had prioritized their personal interests over the economic and geopolitical interests of the United States. Also, according to the Bush administration, House Speaker Nancy Pelosi altered the previously accepted House rules so she could postpone a vote on Colombia. If this ruling was to stand, it would end the pact and most certainly harm American employees and small company owners.

To make the President's tax relief permanent, Congress was to take action. The President had signed into law tax cuts totaling more than $1.3 trillion over the last seven years. The 10 percent individual income tax bracket, the elimination of the marriage penalty, and the reduced rates on ordinary income, capital gains, and dividends would all expire at the end of 2010 unless Congress took action. As a result, the economy would suffer, and 116 million taxpayers could incur an average tax increase of $1,800, it appeared.

The administration wanted Congress to assist American small businesses in navigating the challenging periods and maintain competitiveness going forward.

Legislation on responsible housing could be passed by Congress. This contained bills to update the Federal Housing Administration, change how Fannie Mae and Freddie Mac act governed, and enable State housing organizations to refinance subprime loans with tax-free bonds.

Congress needed to concentrate on increasing access to and affordability of healthcare. All Americans could be able to take advantage of the tax break currently only available to individuals who obtain health insurance from their employment. Thus, Congress could establish a standard deduction for health insurance.

To ensure that our workforce was equipped for occupations in the twenty-first century, Congress could play a role. The President would keep working on a package that he could sign into law to enhance and reauthorize Trade Adjustment Assistance with leaders in both parties. The administration could use its administrative authority to reinforce and improve the No Child Left behind Act until Congress reauthorizes it, giving a new generation the tools they needed to compete and thrive.

The labor movement was founded on the ideas of freedom and choice, which Congress should reaffirm. In order to deny workers their fundamental right to cast a secret ballot while deciding whether to organize a union or stay unaffiliated, Congress could draft a card check styled legislation. The law was said to contradict the foundational tenets of our democracy and exposes workers to intimidation. If this law was to makes it to the President's desk, he was to veto it.

The administration touted how it has taken steps to give the economy a crucial boost.

The President signed a bipartisan stimulus package in February with the intention of reviving the economy. It would take some time for these improvements to be reflected in our nation's economy as a whole. According to many outside experts and the President's economic advisors, the stimulus would start to have a significant effect in the third quarter, which started in July. By giving tax refunds to more than 130 million American households, the economic growth package would increase the purchasing power of American consumers. The rebates would restore as much as $600 to individuals, $1,200 to married couples, and $300 to each kid who qualified. In a few weeks, the tax refunds would begin to be distributed, and a family of four would be eligible for a $1,800 tax refund.

Still Demonstrating Worthy Legacy

Regardless of the challenges and obstructions, the SBA was a reputable organization. Its track record of achievement was proof that small enterprises and communities needed its help. More than anything else, the SBA had assisted small businesses in maintaining their valuable economic contributions, such as the creation of new jobs, tax-paying residents, and, frequently, competitiveness on an international scale. For instance, the SBA offered around 17,000 loans to new businesses in 1999. Even though this only applied to 2 percent of the 887,000 new enterprises that were founded in that year, this percentage was crucial. It had to do with the fact that almost 750,000 small companies shut down in a given year out of the approximately 900,000 that started up each year.

Chapter 16:
Modern Practices, Then and Now Powers

The ways in which this particular organization handles its loans are of utmost significance. The Small Business Administration has worked with 7,000 different banks, some of which provide aid during natural disasters. This has had a positive effect on the economy of the United States of America. According to the results of the SBA's fiscal year 1999, the organization granted loans totaling close to one billion dollars. This was used to finance the reconstruction of homes as well as loans to businesses, which ultimately resulted in the preservation of at least 35,000 jobs. These were persons who had a good chance of losing their jobs and becoming people who did not pay taxes. The same year that it made these loans, it had such programs as the 7(a) program and the 504 programs. It contributed to the creation of 450,000 additional jobs. Because of this, the SBA is now recognized as one of the most successful community assistance organizations around.

With offices in every state of the United States, Guam, and Puerto Rico, the Small Business Administration (SBA) has a significant footprint. Small businesses are responsible for around 47 percent of all sales in the United States, and they have employed approximately 53 percent of the private workforce at times. Even more essential are the contributions made by the SBA to individuals who have traditionally been excluded from the availability of private lenders, such as women and minorities. Between 1987 and 1997, the number of women-owned firms climbed by 89 percent, while the number of minority-owned enterprises as a whole increased by around 168 percent. Indeed, the actions taken by the SBA have many convincing illustrations just like these. Since the beginning of the SBA defense, there have been consistent supportive activities recorded just like those mentioned. Even if financial institutions are able to achieve the same levels of financial clout as the SBA, it will take them a significant amount of time and effort to achieve the same level of background and useful economic expertise as tried administrators like the SBA has. When evidence such as this is produced, there is a good chance that the Small Business Administration will survive the dangers posed by current presidential administrations and those administrations to come. The United States of America requires an agency that has developed over the years and has demonstrated its ability to adapt to new circumstances.

It is estimated that approximately 55 percent of all new business ideas in the United States originate in the small business sector. According to reports, this represented twice as many ideas generated by each individual compared to a big company. The United States hopes to continue to retain its constant lead in the world by embracing this type of innovation. The Small Business Administration (SBA) will, according to all available historical evidence, play a significant role in bolstering the country's business expertise for many years to come.

References

Works Cited

Econstor.eu, <u>Why Have Lending Programs Targeting Disadvantaged Small-Business Borrowers Achieved So Little Success in the United States? IZA DP No. 5212 September 2010, Timothy Bates, Magnus Lofstrom, Lisa Servon</u> referenced July 8,2024 https://www.econstor.eu/bitstream/10419/46043/1/659649403.pdf

Wikipedia, <u>National City Cooporation</u> July 7, 2024 https://en.wikipedia.org/wiki/National_City_Corp.

PBS.org <u>WGBH American Experiences Features establishing National Bank</u> July 7, 2024 https://www.pbs.org/wgbh/americanexperience/features/establishing-national-bank/

SBA.gov. <u>Evaluation of SBA 7(a) Loans Made to Poultry Farmers</u> July 7, 2024 <u>https://www.sba.gov/sites/default/files/2019-07/SBA-OIG-Report-18-13.pdf</u>

SBA.gov, <u>U. S. Small Business Administration</u> July 7, 2024 <u>https://www.sba.gov/</u>

U. S. Small Business Administration, <u>Office of the National Ombudsman</u> July 7, 2024 <u>https://www.sba.gov/about-sba/oversight-advocacy/office-national-ombudsman</u>

U.S. Census Bureau, <u>Survey of Business Owners (SBO) - Business Owners: 2002 Visualizations</u> June 30, 2024 https://www.census.gov/library/visualizations/2006/econ/2002-sbo-business-owners.html

U.S. Bureau of Labor Statistics, <u>TED: The Economic Daily, Self - employment rates, 1948-2003, August 24, 2004</u> June 30,2024 https://www.bls.gov/opub/ted/2004/aug/wk4/art02.htm

EN.Wikipedia.org <u>Wiki PNC Finantial Services</u> April 15, 2024 https://en.wikipedia.org/wiki/PNC_Financial_Services

SBIC law <u>About Us</u> April 15, 2024 https://www.sbiclaw.com/about-us/

Guidant Financial <u>SBA Loan Process Review</u> April 15, 2024 https://www.guidantfinancial.com/sba-loan-process-overview/

ACSS.org UK <u>What is Social Science</u> April 15, 2024 https://acss.org.uk/what-is-social-science/

SBA.gov <u>Funding Programs Loans</u> April 15, 2024 https://www.sba.gov/funding-programs/loans

EEOC <u>Federal Sector Small Business Administration</u> (SBA). April 14, 2024 https://www.eeoc.gov/federal-sector/small-business-administration-sba

SBA.gov <u>About SBA-SBA - Locations Headquarters – Offices Office Small Business Development Centers</u>. April 14, 2023 https://www.sba.gov/about-sba/sba-locations/headquarters-offices/office-small-business-development-centers

Ballotpedia.org <u>U. S. Small Business Administration</u> April 14, 2024 https://ballotpedia.org/U.S. Small Business Administration

SBA.gov <u>Article November 21, 2023 SBA Announces Biden-Harris Administrations Progress Small Business Lending Lend Year Capital Program.</u> April 14, 2023 https://www.sba.gov/article/2023/11/21/sba-announces-biden-harris-administrations-progress-small-business-lending-end-year-capital-program

The Whitehouse <u>Fact sheet ahead of Small Business Saturday Biden Harris Administration announces latest steps to support small businesses</u>. April 14, 2024 https://www.whitehouse.gov/briefing-room/statements-releases/2023/11/21/fact-sheet-ahead-of-small-business-saturday-biden-harris-administration-announces-latest-steps-to-support-small-businesses/

Kenton, Will Small <u>Business Administration (SBA): Definition of what it does.</u> April 14, 2024 https://www.investopedia.com/terms/s/small-business-administration.asp

Nickerson, Charlotte <u>Simply Psychology: Emile Durkeim's Theory.</u> March 30, 2024 www.simplypsychology.org/emile-durkeims-theories.html

Bean, Jonathan J. <u>Big Government and Affirmative Action: The Scandalous History of the SBA</u>. University of Kentucky Press Books Review. 1-2.1 Nov.2001. www.uky.edu/university press/books/biggov.

Canning, Eileen. "SBA to Test Web Loan Guarantee System." <u>American Banker</u>. Vol.165.Issue 160.p3,1/3p. August 21 2000.1-2.EBSCOhost. November 3 2001. Keyword: SBA.

Clinton, Bill, and Al Gore. "The New SBA, Reinventing Service to the Small Business Community." <u>National Performance Review</u>. Government Publication. June 12 1995.11-37.

Gordon, Jennifer. "Senator to Propose Restoring SBA Funds." <u>American Banker</u> Vol. 166.Issue 67. p. 4 1/3p. April 6 2001. 1-2. EBSCOhost. November 3 2001.Keyword: SBA.

Johnson, William C. <u>Public Administration: Policy, Politics and Practice</u>. 2nd ed. Boston: McGraw Hill,1996.184-185.

Kline, Alan. "From Private Sector, A Challenger to SBA." <u>American Banker</u>. Vol. 166. Issue 109.p1,2p 1c,1bw. July 7 2001.1-2. EBSCOhost. November 3 2001. Keyword: SBA.

Olson, Scott. "Black businesses are getting unexpected SBA visits." <u>Indianapolis Business Journal</u> November 3 2001. Keyword: SBA.

Wernner, Gretchen, "SBA wants to give business a voice concerning gov't regulations." <u>Business Journal Serving Fresno & the Central San Joaquin Valley</u>. Issue 322757. p3,2p. April 9 2001.1-2. EBSCOhost. November 3 2001.Keyword: SBA.

Zion, Lee. "SBA Helps Firms Fight Drugs in the Workplace." <u>San Diego Business Journal</u>. Vol. 21.Issue 50.p36,1/2p. December 11 2000.1-2. EBSCOhost. November 3 2001.Keyword:SBA.

US Small Business Administration Office of Advocacy. <u>Energy and Transportation</u>. November 19 2001.1-3. www.sba.gov/advo/research/summaries/catalog/chapt10.html.

U. S. Small Business Administration. <u>FY2001-2006 Strategic Plan</u>. 2-10. November 19 2001. www.sba.gov/strategicplan.pdf.

USSBA. <u>History of SBA: 47 Years of Service to America's Small Business</u>. May 5 2001.1-3.3 Nov.2001. www.sba.gov/aboutsba/sbahistory.doc.

US Small Business Administration: Regulatory Enforcement Ombudsman. <u>Major Developments Benefiting Small Business Related to Regulatory Compliance: Chronology of the last Twenty Years</u>. November 19 2001. www.sba.gov/ombudsman/develop.html.

US Small Business Administration. <u>Regulatory Fairness Fact Sheet</u>. November 19 2001. www.sba.gov/ombudsma/regfairfacts.html.

US Small Business Administration Office of Advocacy. <u>Small Business Economic Indicator for 1999</u>. Washington, DC. 24 Aug.2001.10, fig.2.4.19 Nov.2001. www.sba.gov